P.A.W.S.

Post-Acute Withdrawal Syndrome

One Man's Journey for His Daughter

Josh Kowalczyk

Farabee Publishing
Arizona

This book is the memoirs of Josh Kowalczyk. These are his words and thoughts while going through his withdrawal program.

Farabee Publishing
Chandler, Arizona, 85224
www.Farabeepublishing.com

Printed in the United States of America

Book Cover designed by: David Mor

ISBN: 978-1-68489-364-5

Forward by Publisher

The next time you stop off at the bar after work and have that drink. Ask yourself 'Do I need this?'

When you get home and the first thing you do is grab that beer from the refrigerator, mix a drink, or light up a marijuana joint look at it in your hand and ask, 'Do I need this?'

If the answer is YES. You need to read this book.

The first part of the book is educating everyone on Post-Acute Withdrawal Syndrome (P.A.W.S.) and the symptoms.

The second part of the book is in Josh's words. How he was feeling and the affect that being an addict has had on his life.

His message is strong and needed today.

We are all addicted in some way. Maybe not to drugs and deal with substance abuse but we like the high we get when we accomplish a task, get a new project or when something special occurs in our lives.

We do not see the dopamine rush, we do not recognize the emotional and physical changes because we do not see them as that. We accept them as feelings because we have achieved something or received an unexpected gift.

Question your doctor on what drugs you are taking and if they are necessary. Learn the side effects of all drugs.

I have learned a lot while putting this book together. I hope you read it and learn a lot more about how your body reacts to normal reactions, drugs, and alcohol.

Listen to what Josh has to say and learn about P.A.W.S.
Post-Acute Withdrawal Syndrome

Table of Contents

Forward by Publisher

The next time you stop off at the bar after work and have that drink. Ask yourself 'Do I need this?'

When you get home and the first thing you do is grab that beer from the refrigerator, mix a drink, or light up a marijuana joint look at it in your hand and ask, 'Do I need this?'

If the answer is YES. You need to read this book.

The first part of the book is educating everyone on Post-Acute Withdrawal Syndrome (P.A.W.S.) and the symptoms.

The second part of the book is in Josh's words. How he was feeling and the affect that being an addict has had on his life.

His message is strong and needed today.

We are all addicted in some way. Maybe not to drugs and deal with substance abuse but we like the high we get when we accomplish a task, get a new project or when something special occurs in our lives.

We do not see the dopamine rush, we do not recognize the emotional and physical changes because we do not see them as that. We accept them as feelings because we have achieved something or received an unexpected gift.

Question your doctor on what drugs you are taking and if they are necessary. Learn the side effects of all drugs.

I have learned a lot while putting this book together. I hope you read it and learn a lot more about how your body reacts to normal reactions, drugs, and alcohol.

Listen to what Josh has to say and learn about P.A.W.S.
Post-Acute Withdrawal Syndrome

Table of Contents

Introduction

Most addicts don't know about Post-Acute Withdrawal Syndrome (P.A.W.S.), until they have to quit substance abuse on their own, whatever reason they are quitting!!

P.A.W.S.sounds like cute little P.A.W.S. on a puppy or kitten, but P.A.W.S. will play with you before you play with P.A.W.S.!

Researchers say this is why most people relapse. They get through 1, 2, 3 months of treatment then goback to reality of life's issues and are still struggling with the 10 symptoms they have in P.A.W.S.: depression, insomnia, agitation, anhedonia, etc.

Which means a brain with little or no pleasers because you're now dealing with the psychological and emotional stages in recovery that science says can take 6 months to 2 years to overcome.

P.A.W.S. and anhedonia usually peak between 3 and 6 months and usually go away in a year because the first year your experiencing your 1st Christmas, 1st birthday, 1st new year's now in sobriety.

****

(Anhedonia. an·he·do·ni·a means the inability to feel pleasure.)
(Sobriety. so·bri·e·ty is the state of being sober.)

****

Neurons that once fired together will rewire together in time, but it's not an overnight process. It's like if you have knocked down a brick wall and all the wires were hanging out.

It would take time to put it back together. Our brains are the most amazing thing on the planet. When we go into recovery our brains start healing itself from day one in a process called neuroplasticity.

****

(Neuroplasticity. neu·ro·plas·tic·i·ty is the ability of the brain to form and reorganize synaptic connections, especially in response to learning or experience or following injury.)

****

Our neurotransmitters are not working properly because of the prolonged drug and alcohol use. The good news is that our brains do heal and with abstinence we can get that natural rewards of the natural dopamine feeling back.

****

(Dopamine. do·pa·mine is a compound present in the body as a neurotransmitter and a precursor of other substances including epinephrine).

(Epinephrine. ep·i·neph·rine is another name for adrenaline.)

****

Our brains are remarkable even your liver is a remarkable organ that can return to normal even after decades of misuse.

Our liver has the same enzymes as a lizard's tail. You chop half of it off and it is capable of growing right back in time!

Going back to the brain. We now know, just in the mid-90s, that our brains are remarkable. We used to think we are born with one brain and when damage is done it stays damaged. So glad we're not trying to get sober in the Woodstock age.

Emotional pain is worse than physical pain and when we're doing drugs and alcohol we are essentially slowly torturing ourselves. I could only imagine addicts trying to quit back then, getting past the acute stage, then not knowing, if they got a little further into they're recovery, that the magic mind would come back and eventually the depression, and anhedonia would be lifted.

It was not until the mid-90s, science believed when we sleep our brains and bodies lay dormant, this is not the case, researchers proved when we sleep, in recovery, our brains are basically doing pushups, and detoxing, rewiring, and healing more than we think!!

You probably won't feel better every day, but every month you will. Remember it's a 12 step/12-month program that takes more time than most people think. P.A.W.S. is the second and final stage that most people don't know about and research shows that's when most people relapse.

When we recover on a cellular level it can take months or even years past addiction for our bodies to become smart and sexy in slow-briety. Looking at pictures before and after the proof is in the pudding.

For instance, the faces of meth. Our bodies are a remarkable specimen and with exercise, plenty of water, and a healthy diet and of course abstinence from the drug or alcohol, we can speed up our recovery and let time start the healing.

Even just starting out with baby steps, putting your running shoes by the front door, knowing you're not even going for a walk tomorrow. If you have to lay around the first couple of weeks or months and sweat it out and rest or maybe take supplements like a multivitamin, or apple cider vinegar with Mother. That has proven in many ways to help detoxify our bodies and lose the excess weight we might have gained in our drinking or smoking weed and eating junk food habits.

Exercise produces natural rewards. Even a slow walk around the block will help in early recovery. Drinking large amounts of water is proven to produce natural dopamine to the brain.

Remember drugs and alcohol is DOPE, short for dopamine!! Drugs and alcohol are like a dopamine loan shark, it might feel great at the moment but eventually will wreak havoc on your brain and nervous system and will take much longer to heal than the temporary high itself.

The moment you stop using the substance it's important to know your mind, body and soul are instantly starting to heal and come back to its original state, but as addicts we want everything now.

'P.A.W.S.' does not work that way. It is a snail-paced process that takes more time than most addicts or even society thinks.

You have to have the attitude of when you plant a seed in the soil, and you look at it a few weeks later and see nothing. Just know that underneath that soil a colorful flower will blossom.

Remember broken crayons all color the same. You have to have a can-do attitude about tomorrow because God's already there.

Basically, focusing in on P.A.W.S., slow-briety doesn't happen overnight, it takes more than just a few months for successful recovery. Chances of staying sober after a year skyrocket.

P.A.W.S. is like an EKG strip, you will have plenty of ups and downs, but in order for your brain to recalibrate itself at a normal baseline level, it takes more time than society knows or accepts for addicts to have a successful recovery!

Learning that addiction is a disease and actually hijacks the brain and makes our liver regenerate 100% of its cells every 300 days, was a turning point in my life!

Habit or Addiction

The debate between habit vs. addiction has become more intense for mental health experts. Adi Jaffe, Ph.D., of Psychology Today analyzed the ability for people to choose their habits or addictions.

"In the end, it comes down to training," Jaffe said. "If we want to end up with a different set of behaviors, we have to understand the mechanisms and processes that got us there and make a change." Although this certainly isn't a definitive end to the debate, it does add a layer of understanding to the difference between addiction vs. habit (Alvena Univ., 2019. Par. 11)

Habit Vs. Addiction: A Checklist

According to Chris Clancy (2021), at the JourneyPure At The River, there are four questions to consider regarding your drug or alcohol use:

- Is your behavior having a negative impact—directly or indirectly—on your life?
- Do you repeatedly put yourself in risky situations?
- When you stop drinking or using for any length of time, do you experience withdrawal symptoms like anxiety or stress?
- Have you taken steps to hide your behavior or have you repeatedly, but unsuccessfully, tried to stop drinking or using on your own?

If you answered yes to any of these questions, you likely suffer from addiction.

National Institute of Health

"A common misperception is that addiction is a choice or moral problem, and all you have to do is stop. But nothing could be further from the truth," says Dr. George Koob, director of NIH's National Institute on Alcohol Abuse and Alcoholism. "The brain actually changes with addiction, and it takes a good deal of work to get it back to its normal state. The more drugs or alcohol you've taken, the more disruptive it is to the brain."

"Brain imaging studies of people addicted to drugs or alcohol show decreased activity in this frontal cortex," says Dr. Nora Volkow, director of NIH's National Institute on Drug Abuse. "When the frontal cortex isn't working properly, people can't make the decision to stop taking the drug—even if they realize the price of taking that drug may be extremely high, and they might lose custody of their children or end up in jail. Nonetheless, they take it."

"Treatment depends to a large extent on the severity of addiction and the individual person," Koob adds. "Some people can stop cigarette smoking and alcohol use disorders on their own. More severe cases might require months or even years of treatment and follow-up, with real efforts by the individual and usually complete abstinence from the substance afterward."

According to Pyramid Healthcare, Inc.

"In behavioral health, the differences between a habit and an addiction can be unclear. Habits can be difficult to break, however, unlike addiction, they typically do not have a negative impact on our ability to function. Addiction is much more powerful. Here are some signs that drug use may be an addiction:" (Pyramid Healthcare, 2016)

- An increase in time spent using drugs
- Difficulty stopping drug use, due to chemical changes in the brain
- Presence of withdrawal symptoms when drug use stops
- Financial, emotional, or social problems associated with drug use
- Lower quality of life

Questions to Ask Yourself

If you're concerned that your habit may be harmful, ask yourself these questions: (Pyramid Healthcare, 2016)

- Have you tried repeatedly and unsuccessfully to break your habit?
- Is your use of drugs or alcohol leading to poor decision-making or risky behaviors?
- Do you find yourself craving drugs or alcohol?
- Do you hide your substance use or defend it to others?
- Is your habit negatively impacting work, school, or relationships?

Your answers may reveal a dependence on drugs or alcohol that requires professional treatment.

Acronyms For Alcohol Addiction And Marijuana Habit

Marijuana – **M**edicinal **A**nd **R**ecreational **I**nformation **J**uveniles **U**nderstand **A**s **N**on **A**ddictive.

Alcohol – **A**lways **L**oosing **C**ontrol **O**f **H**umanity's **O**wn **L**ife.

Habit or Addiction (Marijuana)

Habit's definition is a settled or regular tendency or practice, especially one that is hard to give up.

That being said look at what the individual is looking for. If they are looking for release of anger, stress, life's situation, or other issues they will use a drug that offers them a high. This takes them away from their situation for a while but it is not the cure. It is a moment in time when they do not care where they are or what the situation is.

In order for a person to stop addiction or a habit that offers escape for them, they have to replace the need with something else.

The desire to just quit in any cases is not enough and there are addictions or habits that require help to quit. The time it takes to quit and the complications will depend upon the length of time that the drug has been used as an escape route.

"Duke University study of 496 adult marijuana smokers who tried to quit found that 95.5% of them experienced at least one withdrawal symptom while 43.1% experienced more than one symptom. The number of symptoms the participants experienced was significantly linked to how often and how much the subjects smoked prior to trying to quit" (Hartney, 2021, par.4).

As a result, the diagnostic criteria for cannabis withdrawal is included in the Diagnostic and Statistical Manual of Mental Disorders, fifth edition (DSM-5). (Bonnet, U., 2017).

Bottom Line

Read Elizabeth Hartney's article entitled, *How Long Does Withdrawal From Marijuana Last?* To fully understand the effects of any drug read the latest information and talk about why you are using any drugs.

Look at the resources that are presented on the Resource page. There is more than one answer but the big question is, "Why are you taking drugs."

The question might have a simple answer but the realization is that you are letting a substance the offers you a 'high' control your life.

Take your life back and contact help to realize that you do not have to be addicted or form habits of using a drug to sustain your life.

Realization – You are an Addict

Post-Acute-Withdrawal Syndrome (P.A.W.S.)

What Is P.A.W.S.

To understand Post-Acute Withdrawal Syndrome (P.A.W.S.), one must first understand the two stages of detox or withdrawal symptoms (Parisi, 2020).

The first stage of detox, acute withdrawal, is primarily physical withdrawal symptoms that can last from a few days and up to two weeks.

Acute withdrawal symptoms are the immediate or initial withdrawal symptoms that occur upon sudden cessation or rapid reduction of the use of addictive substances, including alcohol.

Many people seek help through a medically supervised detox or by attempting to quit alone, or cold turkey. Acute withdrawal can produce more dangerous health consequences—even life-threatening complications—if detox isn't completed in a supervised setting.

This is especially true, for example, of individuals who are in the acute withdrawal stage of alcohol, benzodiazepines, and barbiturates, as these substances have increased risk of complications without medical supervision, including seizures or coma.

Due to the wide range of acute withdrawal symptoms that may occur, and the various addictive substances that may be used, it is always advised to seek medical assistance rather than quitting on your own, or cold turkey.

The second stage of detox, known as post-acute withdrawal syndrome (P.A.W.S.) occurs as the brain re-calibrates after active addiction.

****

Unlike acute withdrawal, which is primarily physical withdrawal symptoms, the symptoms of post-acute withdrawal are primarily psychological and emotional symptoms.

****

Depending on the intensity and duration of alcohol or other drug use, post-acute withdrawal is known to last many months.

Post-acute withdrawal symptoms typically last between one to two years; however, the severity and frequency of symptoms tend to dissipate as times goes by without the use of addictive substances.

Post-Acute Withdrawal Syndrome can be not only discomforting, but symptoms can appear sporadically, making P.A.W.S. a driving factor for many individuals to relapse, despite how committed they are to staying clean and sober.

Regardless of the addictive substance(s) used, P.A.W.S. are typically the same for most individuals in early recovery from substance use disorders (SUD).

"**P.A.W.S.** is not an official medical diagnosis and it's not found in the Diagnostic and Statistical Manual of Mental Disorders." There are very few published scientific research studies that even confirm the existence of **P.A.W.S.** and there is a particular lack of any recent research about post-acute withdrawal (Buddy, 2020).

P.A.W.S. refers to any symptoms that persist after acute withdrawal has resolved. It can feel like a "rollercoaster" of symptoms, which come and go unexpectedly.

Each episode of P.A.W.S. can last for a few days, and these can continue cyclically for a year. These symptoms can occur with any intoxicating substance, although Post-Acute Withdrawal Syndrome most often occurs among people discontinuing the following drugs (American Addiction Centers, 2021)

- **Alcohol**: Though people have struggled to end alcohol addiction for much longer, the symptoms of P.A.W.S. were first defined for alcohol use disorder in the 1990s.

  Suddenly stopping alcohol consumption is dangerous, since it can cause delirium tremens (including seizures and psychosis) and can also increase the likelihood of P.A.W.S. (e.g., long-term cravings, exhaustion, and feeling ill).

- **Antidepressants**: While few people abuse these drugs recreationally since they do not cause a rapid intoxication, stopping them suddenly can dramatically change the levels of serotonin and other neurotransmitters in the brain. Since people who struggle with depression are prescribed antidepressants, acute withdrawal will feel like intense depression; unfortunately, this experience could continue for months.

- **Antipsychotics:** These drugs bind to dopamine receptors to decrease hallucinations and delirium. When they are discontinued, especially without a taper, the person could experience withdrawal symptoms like mood swings for months.

- **Benzodiazepines:** Although these medicines help people with anxiety and panic disorders, they are very easy for the brain to develop a dependence on. Most prescriptions do not cover more than two weeks of regular use because they can be addictive. Withdrawal symptoms mimic panic disorders, making it harder to stop taking them. P.A.W.S. symptoms, like insomnia, fatigue, and cravings, can last for months after the physical dependence has ended.

- **Marijuana:** Many people become reliant on marijuana to relax and feel normal.. When they stop taking the drug, they can feel stressed, depressed, and paranoid. One of the most common withdrawal symptoms is insomnia, and without medical help, this could persist and become P.A.W.S..

- **Opioids:** Whether prescription opioids or illicit versions like heroin, these drugs can lead to Post-Acute Withdrawal Syndrome if they are not tapered off properly.
  People who experience the full intensity of acute withdrawal are more likely to develop P.A.W.S., which includes cravings, exhaustion, and cognitive impairment that does not go away for a long time.
- **Stimulants:** Drugs from Ritalin to cocaine can cause Post-Acute Withdrawal Syndrome if withdrawal is not managed appropriately. Although a person taking stimulants may experience negative side effects like paranoia, twitching and tremors, and aggression. The opposite symptoms – extreme fatigue, deep depression, and physical weakness – can be harder to manage psychologically.

As acute withdrawal symptoms fade, P.A.W.S. may be an issue for people in recovery. These symptoms, too, will vary in characteristic and degree based upon a number of factors. In general, however, many clients in recovery report experiencing some or many of the following post-acute withdrawal symptoms: (American Addiction Center, 2021)

- Irritability and hostility
- Depression
- Anxiety
- Mood swings
- Low energy and fatigue
- Sleep disruption, including insomnia
- Limited ability to focus or think clearly
- Lack of libido
- Inexplicable chronic pain

Theories about the causes of P.A.W.S. include: (American Addiction Centers, 2021)

Homeostatic Adjustment: A person's physical dependence on drugs or alcohol leads to brain chemistry changes over time; when the body does not have the chemical flowing in, triggering neurotransmitters and endorphins to release, it cannot reach equilibrium on its own.

The brain can take a long time to completely reach homeostasis without chemical help, and this can manifest in mood swings, exhaustion, cravings, and other psychological signs during P.A.W.S..

Physiological Adaptations: Other parts of the body may be used to an influx of drugs to regulate functions like digestion or hormones. Withdrawal symptoms reflect this – for example, nausea, stomach cramps, and diarrhea are common opioid withdrawal symptoms. But sometimes, these can take longer than two weeks to return to normal. For example, heart rate may be more rapid after overcoming an addiction to CNS depressants.

****

(CNS is Central Nervous System. These are medicines that include sedatives, tranquilizers, and hypnotics. These drugs can slow brain activity, making them useful for treating anxiety, panic, acute stress reactions, and sleep disorders.)

****

Stress: It is psychologically stressful to stop taking a drug, especially for people who try to do it cold turkey or alone. This stress may lead to relapse, or it could lead to a prolonged experience of withdrawal symptoms, as the individual tries to make sense of life without drugs or alcohol.

Habit: Part of rehabilitation is to retrain behaviors and responses to drugs or alcohol. Recovering heroin addicts mention the ritual of cooking and injecting the drug, while people who overcame alcohol use disorder note the loss of social situations.

Returning to habit leads to relapse, but the loss of the habit or tradition can enhance psychological symptoms like depression, cravings, anxiety, or exhaustion, leading to P.A.W.S..

Because P.A.W.S. symptoms are largely psychological and emotional, ongoing support from therapists and counselors is important in reducing the intensity of this experience. Here are steps medical professionals may take to help their clients: (American Addiction Centers, 2021)

- Educate clients about withdrawal and what to expect for recovery.
- Celebrate every accomplished step in the process.
- Encourage patience.
- Find natural ways to help with sleep problems.
- Prescribe exercise and healthy diet.
- Assess potential co-occurring disorders, which may emerge or re-emerge.
- Encourage joining mutual support groups.
- Help to manage impulse control.
- Take self-reported symptoms seriously.

In the first days and weeks following the cessation of drug and alcohol use, individuals may experience acute withdrawal symptoms, which can be more severe for some than others and will vary depending upon the drug of choice among other factors (American Addiction Centers, 2021).

Although withdrawal symptoms are uncomfortable, they typically end after two weeks at most, especially when a medical professional oversees the detox process.

However, some drugs can lead to prolonged or protracted withdrawal, lasting for months and sometimes up to a year.

People who consume a large amount of an intoxicating substance for a long time are more likely to develop this condition, which is called **Post-Acute Withdrawal Syndrome** (P.A.W.S.) (American Addiction Centers, 2021).

"Post-acute withdrawal syndrome (P.A.W.S.) refers to withdrawal symptoms that persist for an extended duration following drug discontinuation. Post-acute withdrawals are most commonly referenced among individuals discontinuing opioids. This is due to the fact that during opiate withdrawal, individuals often endure intense short-term symptoms and think that their withdrawals will be over after they "weather the storm."" (Mental Health Daily, n.d., Para. 1).

If you are experiencing or have experienced Post-Acute Withdrawal Syndrome, it is important to consider the factors that may have influenced its duration. The factors listed may play a role in influencing both the severity and number of symptoms you experience. (American Addiction Centers, 2021).

1. Time Span

In general, the longer the duration over which you've taken a drug, the greater the severity of withdrawal.

In fact, sometimes the recovery period may be longer than the term over which you used the drug.

****

If you've been taking an antidepressant for 10 years, decide to stop, and hope that you'll feel normal in just a couple weeks is completely misguided.

****

Whatever chemical you had been supplying your body with for a long-term will result in a temporary deficiency upon discontinuation.

It can take a while for your body (a complex system) to repair all of the changes that were made by the drug and re-learn how to manufacture an endogenous supply of neurotransmitters, hormones, etc. Those that had taken opioids for a long-term often experience "P.A.W.S." because their body needs to re-learn how to manufacture its own, endogenous endorphins rather than rely on a synthetic drug.

****

(Endogenous. en·dog·e·nous having an internal cause or origin.)

(When endorphin activity is stimulated – either naturally or by chemical means – individuals experience relief of pain and sensations of improved well-being.)

2. Frequency

Most individuals experiencing Post-Acute Withdrawal Syndrome are likely to have taken their drug on a daily basis or multiple times per day. The greater the frequency over which you took a particular drug, the more likely you'll be to experience post-acute withdrawals. Someone who takes a drug once per week has a virtually zero percent chance of experiencing post-acute withdrawals.

3. Dosage

The effect of a drug is often dictated by the dosage administered. Taking the minimal effective dose is much less likely to result in a post-acute withdrawal than taking the maximum dose or a supratherapeutic dose.

Certain drugs like opioids, benzodiazepines, and psychostimulants are associated with rapid-tolerance development.

****

(Stimulant, any drug that excites any bodily function, but more specifically those that stimulate the brain and central nervous system. Stimulants induce alertness, elevated mood, wakefulness, increased speech, and motor activity and decrease appetite.)

****

4. Tapering vs. Cold Turkey

To minimize potential of experiencing Post-Acute Withdrawal Syndrome, it is always recommended to follow a tapering protocol. The speed by which you taper should be calculated based on your individual circumstances, the drug you've been taking, how long you've been taking it, and your dosage.

As a general rule of thumb for antidepressants, dosing should be reduced by 10% per month, sometimes slower or quicker depending on the individual.

5. Individual Factors

In some cases, two people may take the exact same drug, at the same dose, for the same period of time. However, one person may experience a withdrawal period that lasts 3 months, while another may experience a withdrawal period that lasts 9 months. What explains the difference between these two people? Individual factors.

Drugs That Can Cause P.A.W.S.:

Drugs that have a significant effect on brain functioning are most likely to result in Post-Acute Withdrawal Syndrome. That said, theoretically any substance ingested over a long-term could result in noticeable protracted discontinuation effects. Below is a list of the drugs that are most commonly associated with post-acute withdrawals. (American Addiction Centers, 2021).

Alcohol: Protracted discontinuation effects have been associated with alcohol withdrawal since the 1990s.

****

(Protracted withdrawal, strictly defined, is the presence of substance-specific signs and symptoms common to acute withdrawal but persisting beyond the generally expected acute withdrawal timeframes.)

****

Although properly tapering off of alcohol may mitigate the potential of experiencing protracted symptoms, many people report withdrawal symptoms months after their last drink. It may take a while for certain individuals to fully recover following a period of alcohol abuse or chronic alcohol consumption.

Antidepressants: Individuals taking antidepressants may experience post-acute withdrawals, especially if they discontinue "cold turkey." Most popular antidepressants like SSRIs and SNRIs inhibit reuptake of the neurotransmitter serotonin.

This reuptake is helpful over the short-term, but after a while the drug stops working; this is due to tolerance.

When a person discontinues antidepressants, their brain has to deal with the backlash of low serotonin and sort out an antidepressant-induced chemical imbalance – which can take a long time.

****

(SSRI. Selective serotonin reuptake inhibitors (SSRIs) are a widely used type of antidepressant. They're mainly prescribed to treat depression, particularly persistent or severe cases, and are often used in combination with a talking therapy such as cognitive behavioral therapy, CBT.)

(SNRIs Serotonin and norepinephrine reuptake inhibitors ease depression by affecting chemical messengers (neurotransmitters) used to communicate between brain cells. Like most antidepressants, SNRIs work by ultimately effecting changes in brain chemistry and communication in brain nerve cell circuitry known to regulate mood, to help relieve depression.)

****

Antipsychotics: These drugs function primarily as dopamine receptor antagonists, meaning they bind to the receptors and inhibit stimulation from dopamine. This leads to a reduction in many of the positive symptoms of schizophrenia.

They also elicit a broad range of effects on neurotransmission. When discontinued, withdrawal symptoms may linger for months (or years) before a person fully recovers.

****

(Schizophrenia. schiz·o·phre·ni·a, a long-term mental disorder of a type involving a breakdown in the relation between thought, emotion, and behavior, leading to faulty perception, inappropriate actions and feelings, withdrawal from reality and personal relationships into fantasy and delusion, and a sense of mental fragmentation.)

****

Benzodiazepines: These primarily enhance the effect of GABA neurotransmission, leading to sedation and relaxation. Although they are the most potent anxiolytics, tolerance is rapidly established on benzodiazepines, leading users to end up on high doses. Should a person attempt to discontinue, they must taper as to avoid seizures and death. Even after tapering, withdrawal symptoms are often protracted, sometimes lasting years before full recovery is made.

****

(GABA. Gamma-aminobutyric acid is an amino acid that functions as the primary inhibitory neurotransmitter for the central nervous system (CNS). It functions to reduce neuronal excitability by inhibiting nerve transmission.)

****

Opioids: Regardless of whether you used illicit or pharmaceutical opioids, you may experience Post-Acute Withdrawal Syndrome following the acute stage of withdrawal. Although the acute stage of withdrawal is regarded as the most severe, the functional impairment associated with protracted withdrawal may be difficult to cope with. The "P.A.W.S." associated with discontinuation of opioids and opioid-related drugs may be due to reduced endogenous production of endorphins.

****

(Opoid. o·pi·oid, a compound resembling opium in addictive properties or physiological effects.)

****

Psychostimulants: Those using psychostimulants for a long-term often build tolerance, end up taking high doses, and experience acute discontinuation effects. The acute symptoms are often followed by an extended Post-Acute Withdrawal Syndrome that persists for months after their last pill. This is due to downregulation of receptors and low dopamine stores that must be replenished.

It can take a long time before the brain increases dopamine levels and receptor density.

Steroids: Anyone that's been on corticosteroids for a long-term knows that the withdrawal can be serious.

There are people that have taken drugs like Prednisone for years, attempt to discontinue, only to find that they experience protracted withdrawals.

These protracted withdrawals may persist for years, often leading some patients to abandon the idea of considering withdrawal. For more information read various accounts of Prednisone withdrawal.

****

(Corticosteroids. cor·ti·co·ster·oid, any of a group of steroid hormones produced in the adrenal cortex or made synthetically. There are two kinds: glucocorticoids and mineralocorticoids. They have various metabolic functions and some are used to treat inflammation.)

(Prednisone. pred·ni·sone, a synthetic drug similar to cortisone, used to relieve rheumatic and allergic conditions and to treat leukemia).

****

What Causes P.A.W.S.

It is difficult to pinpoint the specifics behind each individual case of Post-Acute Withdrawal Syndrome. Some potential causes include homeostatic adjustment, neural pathway adaptations, neurotransmitter levels, physiological adaptations, receptor densities, and stress. (American Addiction Centers, 2021).

- **Homeostatic Adjustment**: Upon discontinuation of any drug or substance, the body attempts to function without it. It may have become well-adapted to receiving the chemical that it had been getting each day, but when the supply was cut, it still needed to function. It is attempting to restore biological homeostasis, which can take a long-term and be quite uncomfortable.

****

(Homeostasis. ho·me·o·sta·sis, the tendency toward a relatively stable equilibrium between interdependent elements, especially as maintained by physiological processes.)

****

- **Neural Pathways:** The neural pathways that you had used on the drug may be rendered relatively useless without the drug. New neural pathways are formed anytime a stimulus (including a drug is introduced). When the drug supply is cut, these neural pathways become weaker, leading you to form new neural pathways without the chemicals that you've been ingesting.
- **Neurotransmitter Levels:** It is thought that most individuals experiencing P.A.W.S. have abnormal levels of certain neurotransmitters. These may be directly related to the neurotransmitters that were targeted by the drug they had been taking. For example, long-term amphetamine usage may have depleted certain dopamine stores.

****

(Neurotransmitters. neu·ro·trans·mit·ter, a chemical substance that is released at the end of a nerve fiber by the arrival of a nerve impulse and, by diffusing across the synapse or junction, causes the transfer of the impulse to another nerve fiber, a muscle fiber, or some other structure.)

****

- **Physiological Adaptations:** The body is a complex system and to think otherwise is foolish. The longer you've taken a drug, the greater the number of physiological adaptations has taken place. This includes your gut bacteria, hormones, neurotransmitters, digestion, etc. During Post-Acute Withdrawal Syndrome, these adaptations must readjust and revert back to homeostasis, which can take a long time.

****

(Homeostasis. ho·me·o·sta·sis, the tendency toward a relatively stable equilibrium between interdependent elements, especially as maintained by physiological processes.)

****

- **Receptor Densities:** The densities of certain neurotransmitters may have been altered as a result of your drug use. For example, someone taking the drug Adderall may experience a down regulation of dopamine receptors due to excess dopaminergic stimulation while on the drug. It can take an extended period of time before dopamine receptor density increases.

****

(Dopaminergic. do·pa·min·er·gic, releasing or involving dopamine as a neurotransmitter. Drugs with this effect are used in the treatment of Parkinson's disease and some psychiatric disorders; some are subject to abuse.)

****

- **Stress:** One of the biggest culprits for Post-Acute Withdrawal Syndrome is that of stress. Many people become stressed because their withdrawal symptoms are highly severe and protracted, leading them to believe they have a more serious disease. To exacerbate things, their doctor tells them that withdrawal shouldn't last longer than a week or two. High stress can extend withdrawal, impede recovery, and amplify the intensity of symptoms.

P.A.W.S. Symptoms

- **Anhedonia**: Many people report that they don't feel the same interest in life during P.A.W.S. compared to while they were on a medication or even pre-medication.

It is especially common for individuals to experience prolonged anhedonia or inability to experience pleasure during post-acute amphetamine discontinuation. This anhedonia often stems from reduced production of neurotransmitters that help us experience pleasure.

****

(Anhedonia. an·he·do·ni·a, inability to feel pleasure.)

****

- **Anxiety**: It is also very common to experience post-acute anxiety upon discontinuation of any medication. This post-acute anxiety is very common among benzodiazepine users who may note a severe spike in nervousness following medication discontinuation. In the case of benzo users, this is a result of decreased GABA functioning.
- **Cognitive impairment:** Some people feel as if they're experiencing permanent brain damage as a result of the drug that they had discontinued. This is due to the fact that they aren't able to think clearly and their cognitive performance is compromised. Although the cognitive impairment is not usually permanent, it can be frustrating to put up with poor executive functioning for months or years while your brain heals.
- **Concentration Problems**: Most people will note that they cannot organize their thoughts or focus. Their concentration seems as if it has no hope of ever returning.
  This incessant "brain fog" is usually caused by neurotransmitter deficiencies, particularly dopamine. This is especially common among those who've used psychostimulants for a long-term and then discontinue only to find that their concentration is worse than before they took the medication.

- **Cravings**: During the Post-Acute Phase Of Withdrawal, it is very common for people to experience cravings. They may crave the drug that they discontinued because they dislike the way they feel without it. They may also experience psychological cravings if they had withdrawn from one of the most addictive drugs (e.g., heroin). Cravings generally become less frequent the longer a person has remained abstinent from the drug that they discontinued.

- **Depersonalization**: Sometimes depersonalization may last for months or a full year during post-acute withdrawal. This is characterized as feeling unlike your "normal" self. You may feel as if you're completely "numb" or as if your soul has been extracted only to never return. This is a result of neurotransmitter deficiencies and can be exacerbated by stress.

- **Depression**: It is common to experience a severe, moderate, or even low-grade depression during post-acute withdrawal. If you were taking an antidepressant, there are ways to distinguish withdrawal symptoms from the original mental illness returning. Many people will experience some depression during Post-Acute Withdrawal Syndrome, regardless of whether they were depressed prior to using the drug that they've discontinued.

- **Emotional Instability**: You may find yourself increasingly angry or irritable during post-acute withdrawal. This may be related to dysfunctional neurotransmission and stress. If you feel as though every little thing triggers anxiety, anger, or irritability, just know that this is fairly normal. Over time it will usually subside and can be mitigated with stress reduction exercises.

- **Fatigue**: Many people experience such extreme fatigue after withdrawal from a drug, that they may actually fit diagnostic criteria for chronic fatigue syndrome. This fatigue may persist for months following discontinuation of the medication and result in excess daytime sleepiness.

- **Hypochondria**: Since you are experiencing post-acute withdrawals, you may actually become a hypochondriac. Not only are you hypersensitive to every little sensation you experience, but your doctor may have told you that there's "no way you're still withdrawing."
Being told this is harmful due to the fact that it often leads to obsessing over the possibility that you may have some undiagnosed rare disease; after all, you still have these wicked symptoms.

****

(Hypochondriac. hy·po·chon·dri·ac, a person who is abnormally anxious about their health.)

****

- **Hypersensitivity**: Most people will report that lights are still too bright, sounds are too loud, and every tactile sensation is overwhelmingly painful. If you feel hypersensitive and as if you'd rather live in a bubble than function in the "real world" this is normal. Your nervous system is healing and is delicate to every little sensation.
- **Insomnia**: The most common impediment to sleep is that of insomnia. You may experience overwhelming insomnia characterized by an inability to fall asleep at night and/or an inability to stay asleep. As your brain continues to restore neurotransmitters, receptors, and parasympathetic activation, the insomnia should subside.

****

(Parasympathetic activation. The parasympathetic nervous system controls bodily functions when a person is at rest. Some of its activities include stimulating digestion, activating metabolism, and helping the body relax.)

****

- **Memory Impairment**: There is evidence that using benzodiazepines can cause dementia. That said, many people will experience some degree of memory impairment when they discontinue a drug. While memory impairment is most associated with benzodiazepines, it can occur during a protracted withdrawal phase from any drug. Over time, your memory should improve and the impairment will become less noticeable.

- **Motivational Deficits**: Many people experience avolition or lack of motivation to complete work or school-related tasks upon discontinuation of their drug. The avolition may persist for months or up to a year after they've been abstinent. This often goes hand-in-hand with the P.A.W.S. symptom of fatigue.

- **Obsessive-compulsive Behaviors**: Your thoughts may become obsessive and difficult to control. In fact, you may feel as if you've developed OCD during post-acute withdrawals. The obsessive-compulsive thoughts and behaviors may be a result of neurotransmitter abnormalities and are commonly associated with P.A.W.S. stemming from benzodiazepines.

- **Panic Attacks**: Your nervous system feels shredded and you're dealing with cortisol spikes. Your sympathetic nervous system dominating your parasympathetic functioning and epinephrine levels are through the roof. When your sympathetic nervous system is dominant and your neurotransmitters are at suboptimal levels, panic attacks may ensue.

- **Social Withdrawal**: Many individuals withdraw from socializing as a result of post-acute withdrawal syndrome. Not only are they feeling anxious, depressed, emotionally unstable, and tired – they may feel as if they cannot even hold a conversation. Forcing yourself to interact with others in a low stress environment can actually expedite recovery.

- **Suicidal Thoughts**: If you're experiencing suicidal thoughts, it is recommended to work with a professional. A psychotherapist can be great for teaching you how to cope with these thoughts, but further intervention may be necessary. In my own experience, these thoughts were persistent for months after my withdrawal and took a while before they lessened in severity.

P.A.W.S. Treatment

(American Addiction Centers, 2021).

- **CBT**: (Cognitive Behavioral Therapy.) If you are dealing with post-acute withdrawal syndrome, a smart intervention is that of cognitive behavioral therapy. CBT will help you identify dysfunctional thinking and make behavioral changes to optimize your recovery. A licensed psychotherapist or psychologist may also provide you with much-needed emotional support during P.A.W.S..
- **Exercise**: Partaking in light exercise such as daily walking may help speed recovery. Some exercise is known to promote healing, whereas too much exercise (e.g., excessive cardio) is a bad idea and will likely impede recovery.
- **Nutrition**: If you are shoveling down refined grains, processed foods, and sugars – P.A.W.S. may be exacerbated. Eat plenty of vegetables, healthy fats (e.g., MCT Oil), some protein, with some healthy carbohydrates and fruits. Making dietary adjustments can significantly reduce the intensity of your post-acute withdrawal syndrome.
- **Pharmaceutical Drugs**: There may be some pharmaceutical drugs that could be prescribed to help mitigate post-acute withdrawal syndrome. You may want to work with a psychiatrist or specialist to help you come up with a treatment protocol. For example: Flumazenil has been thought to help with protracted benzodiazepine withdrawal and Acamprosate may help with certain post-acute alcohol discontinuation symptoms.

- **Sleep**: It may be tough to sleep during P.A.W.S. as lingering insomnia is a common symptom. There are many natural supplements like melatonin that may provide some benefit. Try to go to bed at the same time each night and wake up the same time each morning – this helps your circadian rhythm.
- **Stress Reduction**: Perhaps the most important treatment for P.A.W.S. is that of stress reduction. If you can manage to reduce your stress level and avoid freaking out each time you notice a symptom, you'll likely have an easier time coping. For stress reduction, I'd recommend using an emWave2 or taking up a meditation practice for 20 minutes per day. This will help shut off your sympathetic nervous system and promote relaxation.
- **Supplementation**: There are many supplements that you could take during P.A.W.S. to help lessen symptoms and expedite recovery. I've written about the best supplements for antidepressant withdrawal, many of which also can be used during withdrawal from other drugs. I'd avoid a multivitamin and focus on nutrition and select supplements that you may need. A blood test may be advisable to help determine the most beneficial supplements.
- **Tapering Protocol**: If you withdrew from a drug too quickly, you may want to go back on the drug, stabilize, and conduct a slower taper. Follow a tapering protocol but adjust based on how you feel. Realize that some discomfort is inevitable with each consecutive dosage reduction. That said, a slower taper has potential to reduce the severity of your P.A.W.S..

How long does P.A.W.S. last

Everyone wants to know how long post-acute withdrawal syndrome will last, but there's no definitive answer. There have been cases of individuals in the comments section of this site reporting that their post-acute withdrawal syndrome persisted for years.

For most people, post-acute withdrawal syndrome will last somewhere between 6 months and 4 years.

What Is Dopamine?

Dopamine is a type of neurotransmitter. Your body makes it, and your nervous system uses it to send messages between nerve cells. That's why it's sometimes called a chemical messenger (Bhandari, 2019).

Dopamine plays a role in how we feel pleasure. It's a big part of our unique human ability to think and plan. It helps us strive, focus, and find things interesting.

Your body spreads it along four major pathways in the brain. Like most other systems in the body, you don't notice it (or maybe even know about it) until there's a problem.

Too much or too little of it can lead to a vast range of health issues. Some are serious, like Parkinson's disease. Others are much less dire.

It's made in the brain through a two-step process. First, it changes the amino acid tyrosine to a substance called dopa, and then into dopamine.

It affects many parts of your behavior and physical functions, such as:

- Learning
- Motivation
- Heart rate
- Blood vessel function
- Kidney function
- Lactation
- Sleep
- Mood
- Attention
- Control of nausea and vomiting
- Pain processing
- Movement

It's hard to pinpoint a single cause of most mental health disorders and challenges. But they're often linked to too much or too little dopamine in different parts of the brain

Drug Misuse And Addiction. Drugs such as cocaine can cause a big, fast increase of dopamine in your brain. That satisfies your natural reward system in a big way. But repeated drug use also raises the threshold for this kind of pleasure. This means you need to take more to get the same high

If anyone who is fighting addiction or has a loved that is either fighting it or are not aware they are addicted: please educate them about P.A.W.S. and let them know it's real.

Knowing about what to expect in the later stages of recovery and the symptoms of P.A.W.S. after the acute stage, will help take the edge off. Knowing this emotionalroller coaster will pass, and all of the 20 symptoms that P.A.W.S. causes, that most people are not aware of, can heighten your chances of a successful sober recovery!!

Part 2: Josh's Memoirs

Introduction

When I was 20, I started making a wage of $5.37 cents, $350 every 2 weeks back in 1995. I would get paid then on the weekends spend most of it on alcohol and marijuana, then eventually even started once in a while drinking during the week.

Marijuana is known as a non-addictive drug and is romanced by society, marijuana anonymous, just like alcohol anonymous, are there for a reason.

I am living proof, as are millions of others that are struggling with the grim reaper, or the green reefer, devil's lettuce. You get the idea. Dr. Drew, who you seeon TV, has helped thousands and thousands of marijuana addicts, especially now that it is a lotstronger these days. Dr. Drew even goes on to say people detoxing from marijuana and alcohol have a harder time healing than those getting off cocaine and alcohol because the brain significantly ages by the potency of the hetero antibodiesthat stick to our neurotransmitters.

****

(Hetero antibodies. Heterophile antibodies are antibodies induced by external antigens (heterophile antigens). For example, in rheumatic fever, antibodies against group A streptococcal cell walls can also react with (and thus damage) human heart tissues.)

****

Marijuana especially causes P.A.W.S. more than other drugs, that's why the relapses for marijuana is so high and is a proven fact.

It can take up to 90 days to flush out of our system. They get stuck in our fat cells and when you fast or even exercise it gets released back into your system, even in slow-briety which causes what they call a phantom high.

I thought vaping was better than smoking the green but vaping is more condensed and released more things in my system so I tested positive 75 days after I quit and 145 days later I am still feeling the effects it caused me.

Learning in time from research and experience, our brains and bodies heal with every breath we take, even our lungs get 20,000 healing breaths a day, and that adds up!!!

Back to my story, at age 20 I made a horrible mistake after a night of drinking and got behind the wheel of a car and got my first DUI.

I had to lose my license, spend time in jail, and loose about a year of salary at the time!! Not knowing that it would not be my first.

Our gut is our second brain and has a lot to do with our emotional health. We actually have millions of neurons in our gut and smoking weed and drinking alcohol plays a huge role in how we feel.

The third would be your heart. I believe we have 40,000 neurons in our heart, and every 7 years our body regenerates 100% of our cells and in sobriety it works 2-fold!!

I was still working at the hospital, working a job that wasn't paying much for years, working in a comfort zone that looking back wasn't comfortable at all. Don't get me wrong. I truly enjoyed patient care but working in a hospital as a tech you're at the bottom of the food chain, working under doctors, nurses, and other health professionals.

Hospitals are usually understaffed, especially in the wintertime. It seemed like snowbirds in October would fly from back east, get on an ambulance and come straight to the hospital and would increase our volume 50%!!

And when you are a patient care tech a lot of the weight would fall on me and I could walk 15 miles in a 10-hour shift!! But as bad as it got I knew I had my marijuana at home. When I felt really overwhelmed I could go and get a 12 pack of beer and drown my pain!

Julie and I were both living at home, as she worked next door in the doctor's business office.

We both had dreams of finally getting a place together but this was in jeopardy because of my addiction to alcohol and pot.

Remember there is no hope with dope, and as we all want to be successful or famous in life I ended up anonymous, LOL. After just getting out of debt from my first DUI, at age 28, I got a second one.

My addiction was making me make decisions I normally wouldn't and started to affect my relationship with Julie.

A few years later I was getting out of DUI debt once again, and I got my third DUI. Around that time, I really knew I had to make a change!!

Julie and I split up and, shortly after that, her mother passed away from lung cancer. I started looking back at that time thinking what drugs and alcohol had cost not only me, but people around me that I truly loved.

A doctor once said, 'You couldn't think of a cancer that was more debilitating than addiction, and in addiction we don't die as fast as we do in the movies.' As I said, it's a slow process that catches up to you in the end. Shortly after her passing I got clean for a short time and at age 38, 13 years ago.

Prayers go up, blessings come down, and there is no hope with dope!!

Back to my story after getting my first DUI, I was still struggling with getting out of debt from the DUI and still going to the bars and in a comfort zone knowing I had alcohol and marijuana as a crutch.

I was working a job as a tech and playing roller hockey for a local team. Our team was called the Boozerz, half the team would show up for a game, at the local rink, half buzzed from either alcohol or pot.

We would play other teams. Firestorm was the local fire department, and even the police had their own team. Boy did they play dirty. I got my worst high stick between the eyes from a cop toward the end of a game that we had already won!! LOL

Everyone in addiction has the opportunity to straighten up and understand you might be bent but not broken.

After Julie and I were back together and I was out of my DUI debt, we finally saved up enough money to buy a house together and we were just starting to get a taste of the good life.

Boy how I was wrong.

Mark Twain once said, 'It's easy to quit I have done it hundreds of times.' I think he was talking about cigarettes, still a drug, and yes it's easy to quit in the early stages.

But in the post-acute stage 2, 3, 4, 5, 6 months down the road, your brain is still feeling the effects of the P.A.W.S., physically, psychologically, emotionally, insomnia, depression etc..

Something isn't right. If they waited just a little longer and let the second stage of the recovery duration happen, that is when the magic in the mind happens. Our natural dopamine, endorphins, serotonin, neurotransmitters all heal at their own pace.

> *Slow-briety is like faith. You have to take that first step without seeing the top step. Just knowing you are on a journey and at the top of that skyscraper you will reach slow-briety.*

They teach in meetings, everyone in slow-briety has not had their best day yet, it is still to come and it's so true. After addiction we are healing until the day we die. Buzz Aldrin, a man who was the second man to walk on the moon, said his greatest achievement in life was his sobriety.

After even getting into trouble with the law, and all the trouble it has caused, it was his destiny to walk on the moon because his grandmother's name was Mrs. Moon. No joke, LOL.

Just like it's your destiny to get sober and all the natural rewards we are meant to have. The important thing is our bodies have an extremely extraordinary way to heal itself, repair itself and get back into being yourself and escaping the depression, anhedonia, and despair that addiction causes.

Knowing that Slow-briety is not a sprint but more a slow-paced marathon that there is a finish line, you can turn that frown upside down in slow-briety

Back to my story. After 6 months we moved into my first home. I knew deep down I wanted to get clean and knew I would suffer in early sobriety. So, I went to a doctor and he mentioned a drug like lorazepam would help with my anxiety and insomnia.

****

(Lorazepam. lor·az·e·pam, a benzodiazepine tranquilizer used especially to relieve anxiety and insomnia and to control epileptic seizures.)

****

While I was trying to give up weed and alcohol, I took one, then took another. One, because of my high tolerance, I was not feeling the effects and I might have even taken too much!! Long story short I had a reaction to them and crashed my car into a parked car up the street from my house and got my fourth aggravated DUI.

The reaction was so bad after getting out of jail hours later, I had my brother bring his Honda over because I thought I needed to check on my car at the junkyard. Just to slam his Honda into a median and ultimately a palm tree, and in that accident I was taken by ambulance to the hospital with a gash on my head just to score my fifth DUI!!

Out of the hospital I remember having suicidal thoughts and almost knew I was about to lose everything. I would go through the motions again, go to tent city jails in Arizona, somehow keep my job, and once again, slowly climb out of DUI debt.

I would always quit for a while once again in the acute stage, the first stage of recovery but couldn't get past that second and final stage of recovery.

P.A.W.S., that's when the magic of slow-briety happens and your neurotransmitters are magically changing. I never gave it time for the brain fog symptoms todissipate. After weeks, a couple of months, I thought that is how I would feel and didn't give my brain time to heal.

I got clean again and once again my demons fed my soul to slowly start using again and thought I was once again a functioning alcoholic who smoked weed on a daily basis. Julie and I always wanted a child and eventually we had to spend thousands of dollars to go through in-vitro, after a few failed attempts I was blessed with the birth of my daughter.

Out of my 8 siblings, none of my brothers had children, a few of my sisters did. Long story short my mother and father got to see their first Kowalczyk grandchild, Gemma Ann Kowalczyk.

I was so proud, but 9 months later is when tragedy struck. It was Halloween of 2017, my mother arrived at noon to babysit Gemma, as Julie went to work.

Julie mentioned how happy my Mom was to watch Gemma and even did a little dance as she walked in the front door!!

I just got my license back from the previous DUI. I remember pulling into my garage at 2:00 pm, just 2 hours after my Mom arrived. I remember I heard Gemma crying and new something was wrong, As I opened the door I saw my mother's body lying face down directly under Gemma and the baby swing.

Gemma was halfway in the swing ready to fall on my Mom's back. I quickly moved Gemma aside and being CPR certified, I called 911 and proceeded to do CPR on my Mom, but she was already gone! It was like coming home to my own haunted house on Halloween.

I remember thinking God made my Mother a hero and put my daughter above her and now my Mom was in heaven.

My mom would have had 14 of us children but had 5 miscarriages, and I knew she was in heaven with them. Just before my Mother's death I got a Shih tzu dog and I named her Ann, after my Mom. Just before my Mother's death she called me and said her parents called her Angel. I changed my dog's name to Angel!

Shortly after my Mom passed away on Halloween of 2017, she was cremated on my birthday November 15, 2017.

After my Mom's death, I went through a major depression and again fell back into my addictions and three years later, my 2 brothers were having trouble with their addictions as well.

They lost their apartment and were living out of a trailer all summer in Arizona with no A/C.

I felt bad for them and helped them anytime I could give them money. This was taking a toll on my relationship with Julie. Then it came to an end one night, June 17, 2020!!

After drinking all day with my brother's, I came into the house and Julie and I started arguing. She was tired of my all-day drinking binges and took over the counter meds to sleep.

She accidentally cut me with the keys she took out of my hand so I wouldn't drive. I looked down, saw blood, and pushed her off of me.

She was on the phone with my sister and after hearing the argument my sister called my other sister and was worried about the altercation.

I asked Julie to watch Gemma while I went across the street to get food, and Julie refused. We live right on a canal and I was worried Gemma would follow me out the door.

So, in my drunken mind I made a horrible decision and brought Gemma with me. It was just across the street.

As I came home minutes later pulling into my driveway I saw a policeman there with my two sisters Kim and Audra, and her husband Sunny.

Now I am facing my 6th aggravated DUI and later to find out domestic violence for pushing Julie off me. They asked if I wanted to press charges on her because she cut me and I refused.

I wanted her to stay there with Gemma only to find out she got a restraining order on me and haven't been to my house since!!

Two months after the incident I received a lawsuit from her and she was going for full custody of my child.

I'm losing my house, car, dogs, and haven't been able to go back home since. I truly loved her and now my addiction has cost me literally everything. She is buying the house out from under me.

I just finished 25 years working at a hospital and now have to pay criminal, custody, and realtor lawyer fees.

I lost my 401k, my house, my car, and my beautiful daughter, I have only seen once for 2 hours a few months ago. It's now 5 months later and I have not even started court for my DUI or custody battle. I lost everything. I am living with my twin sisters up the street practically in the same zip code as my daughter and all I have is my sobriety.

147 Days Clean

The love for my daughter is keeping me strong and being 147 days clean I have hope and the desire to do whatever it takes to stay sober. I just want to go to court and see how much time I have to do and the only thing that matters to me is seeing my daughter again.

I have my sobriety and hope it will make the process a lot easier, knowing that however much time I have to do I will be healing from the inside out.

The cop didn't tell me at the time, at the house, Julie was pressing charges. I knew I was going for the DUI so even though she cut me, when I was asked to press charges on her I refused, not knowing until hours later she was pressing charges on me.

So, she was able to get the restraining order and now I am homeless, waiting for the house to go in her name and not looking good in the custody case being that I drank and drove. Ultimately I lost everything because my brain was hijacked from my addiction.

I am really looking forward to getting all of this behind me and with my sobriety growing stronger every day, week, month, and eventually year's. I hope to get my life on track with my daughter and never go back to those dark days of addiction.

If I can do it through all of this, anyone can do it, it's just mind over matter, no matter what!! I need to learn how to forgive myself, and hopefully in time everything will work out.

> *Learning about P.A.W.S. has given me hope for a future with sobriety, and a healthy, happier, life with my daughter.*

I know she will never see her grandmother again so as her father I need to be here for her and be strong. Somehow I am going to get through this hard time and make up for all the lost time. I am in the middle of what I have gotten myself. It will take time to fix but I am going to stay with it and finish this.

Just knowing what to expect from P.A.W.S. and that there will be hard times like this just makes it 10 times worse. Knowing it's a temporary syndrome and that it will pass and if I just stay strong and sober it will pass really helps. Just knowing that eventually we can get through P.A.W.S. and live a happy sober life!!

I am not going to lie, just after writing this I cried and is very emotional but P.A.W.S. has our brains on an emotional roller coaster and is like an EKG strip with plenty of ups and downs but eventually not like the heart when you flatline.

We have a second chance with our brains because through P.A.W.S. especially, in stressful situations, your brain's healing power is amazing. If you give it enough time it will go back to baseline and get all the natural rewards.

Remembering Those Times of Addiction

When I was about 33, I was trying to shake off addiction. I saw an ad in the paper at the local casino, Fort McDowell. They were hosting fights at the promotions boxing match competition. I was wanting to get sober so bad I thought if I signed up I would get into shape and stop drinking.

My family thought I was nuts and that's how bad I was in the brink of insanity doing the same thing over and over expecting change due to my alcohol and drug use.

My father was worried that I was suffering from some mental illness, drug psychosis. He wanted me to get institutionalized and treated for my mental health. After being there and after tickets were sold, the fight was the next day, I was determined to fight after selling plenty of tickets to friends and family, and coworkers from the hospital.

I didn't want to let anyone down, and somehow being behind locked electric doors, suffering from some kind of drug and alcohol psychosis, I was determined to make the fight. They were giving me medication at the time that was making me even worse and remember just needing to escape knowing the fight was within 24 hours.

I remember following a family member, that was visiting someone, and somehow caught the electric door behind them. I was almost free and determined to make the fight. I got outside somehow and there was the 12-foot wall. I had to climb the tree and remembered looking over the wall and there was an incline of gravel, that I knew if I jumped I would probably not land well, which I didn't.

I slipped and fell on my knees, and cut my knee open, but I was free and found myself running down a canal to freedom.

They have cut down the tree since my escape. My sister called it the Joshua tree!!

I remember making it to a convenient store where I was able to call my brother-in-law to pick me up and remember even smoking weed the day of the fight.

I promised my Dad that after the fight I would go back to the institution. I went through the full 3 rounds of the fight. I remember punches thrown and getting knocked down and getting back up. I didn't even train for the fight, because at the time I was being institutionalized.

He won the decision and looking back I even smoked weed the day of a huge boxing match that I worked so hard to get to. My addiction was running my life at the time and I truly didn't even know it.

Although, for not training and being injured, and smoking weed the day of the fight, I am lucky I didn't get knocked out.

My friends from work even told me I did well.

It could have gone both ways, but even though I lost, I was glad I didn't let anyone down and went right back to the hospital like I promised. I truly think I was suffering from addiction and didn't know how to handle it, making horrible decisions and hurting not only myself but people I love.

> *I wish I never had got caught up in drugs or alcohol, it has taken a toll on my life in so many ways!*

We Have To Forgive Ourselves

After 25 years I learned plenty. I enjoyed helping people so much and now, in recovery myself, I am learning helping others helps ourselves as well, especially in alcohol anonymous.

I really tried to make patients laugh because that's the closest we can get to heaven here on earth, and slow-briety is possible for all addicts. I believe it's just educating people and know it's possibleto feel like new again!!

> *We do things we normally would not do, so in recovery we have to forgive ourselves and moveforward as yesterday is history and tomorrow is a mystery. Today is a present andtomorrow is a gift, and in slow-briety all things are possible.*

After that I continued to get on with my life and continued drinking beer and chasing that dopamine high, at age 25 I met a girl in the cafeteria named Julie, we fell in love but still in my active addiction, I wasn't in a hurry for the picket fence, house, and kids, that wouldn't happen until I was 37 and losing it all through my addiction.

I met Julie in December of 1999 and a couple of weeks later we were at my sister's house at a new year's eve party. As the ball dropped,for the millennium, everyone was shouting and drinking and my Mom looked at Julie and I and we had our first kiss at the 12:00 midnight 2000!!! The millennium just hit. I'm in love, I loved my job, things were looking good. Boy I was wrong.

Addiction has caused me to go to a gated community that I don't want to be in LOL and learning after six DUI's when I drink I break out in handcuffs! LOL.

Josh's Younger Years

I was 7 years old when my father moved my 8 siblings and I from Syracuse, New York to Chandler Arizona. I remember my first cup of coffee around 6 years old and remember the sugar and creammade the caffeine coffee taste so good. If I only knew caffeine was a drug, caffeine, pot, alcohol etc. is dope, in other words dopamine in short!

I remember all of us children, 6 at the time, 3 boys and 3 girls, just like the Brady bunch, piling in a station wagon and driving cross country from snow capital of the world to hot and sunny Arizona.

I remember being a little rascal and writing on a piece of cardboard, hanging out the back of the wagon practically all the way here, saying help us were being kidnapped! LOL

Arriving to Arizona, I remember two things, the tap water tasted like crap and it must have been July or August because I was outside in the backyard at nighttime with no shirt and hot and sweaty, and that doesn't happen in Syracuse.

Later I would learn a lot more about not only myself but addiction!!! Arriving in Arizona my Mom and Dad eventually had three more children, 6 girls and 3 of us boys total. I could never get into the bathroom, and when I did, I would reach for a hairbrush and burn my hand on a curling iron! LOL

My father was a very spiritual man who went to Catholic church every morning sometimes twice a day and hadn't missed church ever. He had a personal commitment to go every day since he was about 33 years old.

He enrolled me and my siblings into a private school and that's where I tasted my first sip of wine! LOL

> *A cool acronym for bible is Basic, Instructions, Before, Leaving, Earth!! We need to take care of our bodies and they will take care of us, especially in SLOW-BRIETY.*

Growing up my Dad had my 2 brothers and I as altar boys. Then I was going to school at St Mary's school and St. Thomas Church.

When I was younger I was very arrogant and as an altar boy my only goal was to make my brother laugh, on the other side of the altar, and just about every Sunday my Dad would scold us both for acting out!

When I was younger I thought there was no God but now that I'm older I know that there is because life is like a vision, and we see and learn as we age vibrantly, and we don't even know who we are until we are close to death!

My Dad was an optometrist who didn't help me physically see but planted a spiritual seed that helped me see!! He probably knew more about the Bible than his own optical.

Growing up down the street from a roller-skating rink, I started skating and eventually going as a regular 5 times a week.

I loved the natural high skating and the music gave me, the natural dope, dopamine that would make me feel the euphoria that I would choose to chase artificially later in life.

I started a paper route at age 11 and eventually started selling the paper door to door. Not to pat myself on the back, but me and another boy named Buddy always had more orders than anyone. Not only in our district but all of the 8 to 10 Van's carrying 8 to 10 children a piece.

I remember chasing that natural dopamine rush of trying to hit my nightly bonus, or even just taking us out to pizza and free video games.

I still have golden plaques for my sales accomplishment never knowing that dopamine was the culprit. Learning from research our bodies need 3 things to survive food, water, and dopamine!!

First Marijuana Joint

I remember my first drag of a marijuana joint. It's one of those things you always remember, kind of like 9/11!! I was behind Skateworld and remember feeling the artificial dopamine flooding my brain. I was in no pain not knowing the addiction is like emotionally terrorizing oneself, and with slow-briety we can get back to a place we thought was not possible.

After attending St Mary's private school, I started going to a public school, and that's where I was initially introduced to alcohol, and cigarettes. I started smoking a little more pot than I should have.

Even though I thought I was a functioning addict, making the honor roll, and even my junior year was the Male student of the year in the 'Yes To Success Program.'

I still have the golden plaque as well!! LOL. I didn't know what addiction would cost me!! At age 20 I started working at Chandler regional hospital, I worked my way up as a Patient Care Tech!!

I enjoyed helping patients and family members. I was like the jokester in the recovery room. I would walk to the blanket warmer as it looked like a refrigerator, turn to the patient, and say 'want a beer?', then they would go from cold pain to laughter every time, and that was just one of my jokes!!

In my 25 years working at the hospital, I truly loved to make the patients laugh especially the really sick patients because our emotions are everything.

> *In healthcare and slow-briety, emotionally sick people are also physically ill people and addiction is a stigma that really needs to be addressed in society.*

From that time up until my arrest date in 2020, Julie and my relationship really started to take a turn at that point but we tried to hold it together for Gemma's sake, but addiction got the best of me.

During my alcohol and drug experience, I knew after a while especially in my 30 years I knew my head wasn't right. My neurotransmitters were under some kind of drug alcohol psychosis. I used to tell people I have a condition C.D.O. They would say, 'oh yeah what is that?' O.C.D but I like to spell it in alphabetical order!! LOL. Now I am going into the D.O.C (Department Of Corrections), because of my substance use.

In the ages of people between 20 and 64 years old!! It's an epidemic!!

I moved to an apartment in a lesser area and I didn't want anything to happen for my daughter's sake. Being that she was already established on a nice area in a house, by a canal with ducks, and just looking over the back fence a farmer had cows to look at, it was a really nice area. I truly didn't want to be selfish and make her move!

Josh And Joey

Joey and I were really close growing up, we both were altar boys at St. Thomas church for years and went to a Catholic private school at St. Mary's.

We both battled our own addictions on and off and a couple years ago before my Mom died he did get clean. Mom was so proud. My Mom got to see him sober, but then again fell back into addiction.

Joey was one of the biggest hearted people I know and would do anything for anyone. Just weeks before the hit and run accident that took his life, he took time off from work, to help me pick up a few large breakable Disneyland items that Ibought from a gentleman. I just hope he is at peace with my Mom in Heaven.

He tried so hard off and on, trying to battle his demons and just like me, always found a way back to addiction. He was involved in a hit and run accident. This happened 12 hours and 15 minutes ago from my writing this. My Dad was yelling at my front door, 'Joey is dying and he's calling the priest for his last rights.'

We raced to the hospital, where I worked exactly one year ago, and my healthcare family I worked with for years, said they got his pulse back a couple times. Leala, the OR nurse and trauma doctors said he passed away on the operating room table.

I'm 9 months and 9 days sober and for my brother's memory I need to stay sober. I can't even stay strong because I'm not right now. Towards his last few years because of addiction, we both were close, but addiction definitely made us butt heads plenty of times.

I love you so much Joey, and I can't even see what I'm writing because I am crying. I just wish I had helped him more towards the end and naturally just mad at myself for not going 100% to help him say sober.

My religious father is at St Ann's, as I just left him there, and will be there praying for my brother and his son and I just hope my Mom is in heaven welcoming him and hugging him with our savior Jesus Christ, The Prince of Peace!!

I Love You My Little Brother Joseph Theodore KOWALCZYK.

> *People in addiction need to stop and put their sobriety in motion, just like this only picture I have of my brother and I. Life is too short to suffer from addiction.*

This is Joey and me 22 years ago. My sister had to take a photo in motion for school.

I know my father forgives the driver of the hit and run, but I'm at the moment, not strong enough to forgive him. but I need to stay sober through such a tragic time for my daughters future.

My mind has been racing all day and still in and out of shock, half of me wants to take a run in this Arizona heat to destress. The other half is telling me that would be selfish.

His heart stopped today.

Why should I make mine anyhealthier. My mind is really playing tricks on me and I believe it's just another and the worst P.A.W.S. chapter or jump I need to get over.

My brother had the most beautiful smile you can ever imagine and I pray my Mother is witnessing that right now.

As my whole family mourns him and is saying there he goes. My mother and Jesus Christ is saying here he comes!!!

Josh On Specific Drugs - Marijuana

Thirty years ago, when I was introduced to marijuana it was still considered a street drug and less socially accepted but definitely still romanticized as not as harmful as other drugs.

I started slow,and really enjoyed it and didn't realize just how much it affected my motivation and how routinely smoking it, 30 years later I'm smoking from dusk till dawn. Looking back that I was literally a slave to it.

If I went somewhere I needed to go, if I was running low on my stash I would make sure I bought some before running out. Even without it I didn't have much of an appetite. In words, I was addicted.

> *In the future, if I found my daughter smoking a joint, a million things would be going through my head knowing what I know about it and the time and money and emotional terrorism it has costed me.*

Now that it is not only more socially accepted but 10 times more potent, I can be a very naturally motivated guy, but smoking weed really slowed me down.

Message To My Daughter

My daughter is everything to me. Knowing she has my gene's, I know if she smoked it she would learn to possibly enjoy it.

But the risk is not worth the reward.

> *Getting the munchies and having the giggles for a couple of hours, the feeling tired and depressed and putting harmful substances into your natural body just isn't worth it. I think there's a lot more to life than smoking weed every day.*

And so many more younger people are being introduced and influenced to smoke it but don't know just how much it has the potential to slow you down much less become habitforming.

There is a reason Marijuana Anonymous exists, and more younger people are joining because they eventually got addicted and are having a hard time quitting. I just hope my daughter has bigger plans in life and not slowing down because she's dealing with marijuana motivational terrorism.

At 46 years old, and yes it took me this long to figure out, marijuana unlike alcohol, it's not what you did or didn't do the night before but what you did or didn't do the last 25 years smoking pot.

> *My daughter at age 4 soon to be 14. Now that marijuana is legal and so much more socially accepted, it's a big concern of mine.*

I just want you to understand that we have our own cannabinoid system, natural rewards system. I know smoking marijuana definitely lowers your IQ, and makes you tired coming down, and I just hate to see my daughter feel she needs a substance to feel better and survive.

Bottom line, too much marijuana is known to cause Anhedonia and I experienced it, and still healing from it 11 months later, and I would hate to see her go through what I went through.

I procrastinated about quitting for years, always say 'oh maybe I will quit at the end of the month.' I learned that was like saying I will quit on the 32nd, that day would never come. I might go a few days if not weeks, sometime a few months always coming back to it, never taking the time to let the full duration of P.A.W.S. to fully heal. I wasn't aware of SLOW-BRIETY.

Extra Things About P.A.W.S.

Julie and I separated for a about a year and now we are working things out but during those months of not seeing Gemma it was hard.

I just hope my sobriety helps me though my custody and DUI case. I promised my Mother and daughter and myself I will never do drugs or alcohol again. I am really looking forward to healing up from the inside out.

I am looking at prison as a dopamine detox, and to come out and be the best father I can ever be. I am starting to feel the brain fog lift, and just know sobriety will get me through this tuff time.

I will not give 99% anymore because you get back 0%, this time I will give 100% and hopefully get 100% in slow-briety.

I know I am still just barely halfway through P.A.W.S.. With all these new problems, I caused myself and my family, it intensifies the symptoms of P.A.W.S.. But just knowing and educating myself about the second and final stage of P.A.W.S. helps to stay 100% on track. I know I still have months of healing to do and a lot of work ahead of me.

Jail time, money to lawyers, DUI fines, plenty of classes, eventually losing my driver's license, and getting the interlock. I have hoped my natural rewards, my life with my daughter, and finding a good job, will make a huge pivot in my life.

After doing CPR on my mother, I have trouble doing my CPR classes. It brings me back to that moment every 2 years, so I will be getting a new job, not in healthcare. In prison I hope to be healing from inside out and with slow-briety. I will have hope for the future, and not to beworried about tomorrow because God is already there!!

Looking back, I tried in so many ways to get sober. I went through so much and always found myway with the fight of battling addiction.

I am 20 pounds lighter and my head is a little clearer. I will promise Gemma with the best gift I could ever give her is my true self in sobriety and remain sober for the rest of my life and live our lives happily ever after!

How I'm getting through this dealing with P.A.W.S. I don't know. But knowing what to expect and educating myself about P.A.W.S. is the only way I could ever have a chance and focus on my emotions and know that this emotional pain will eventually be lifted.

If I can do it through all of this, I just hope anyone battling addiction, just battle through it.

Be patient and know that life will throw challenges at us and its ultimately how we handle them and with sobriety it will make it that much easier and that anything is possible!!

11 Months Clean

Today is literally January 27th and I just got the news from my sister that I will see my daughter for the first time in months. As I finish this, it's funny how God has such a sense of humor, and I just hope Saturday will be the best day for three hours of my life.

P.A.W.S. is really affecting me at the moment with these circumstances, but I will stay 100% committed knowing I am getting better and stronger every day with my slow-briety and knowing P.A.W.S. will eventually pass!

A very high percent of addicts never knew their true potential. Many became very successful moving on as entrepreneurs, whether it's starting their own business or chasing their own dreams simply using their natural God given talents, using their own dopamine, and knowing they don't have to live that way anymore!!

Simply because addicts are always chasing that high. When they get sober they can rebuild their life. I know I didn't hit rock bottom, but 6 feet under. I am still digging my way up and breaking through the rock and building my rock-solid foundation ground up and with sobriety anything is possible!!!

If anyone who is fighting addiction or has a loved one please educate them about P.A.W.S..

Let them know it's real and knowing about just what to expect in the later stages of recovery and the symptoms of P.A.W.S. after the acute stage.

It will help take the edge off knowing this emotionalroller coaster will pass. Let them know all of the 20 symptoms that P.A.W.S. causes, that most people are not aware of and make their chances possible of a successful sober recovery!!

You just live every day. Say 'I will give it up tomorrow,' then finally you look back and think of all the time, money and problems addiction has caused.

I used to think when I ran out of marijuana and I didn't feel like myself, in my younger years, I thought it was normal to feel like shit not knowing I was detoxing off marijuana and simply not giving it enough time.

> *I wish I knew about P.A.W.S. and this is when weed was way less powerful. I am so concerned about today's youth and know that people need to educate themselves about marijuana and P.A.W.S. and know what they are getting into, and it could cause problems later in life and it's just a matter of time!!*

And eventually if and when you decide to give it up it will take more time than most people think to sober up and feel better. It is a drug that stays in your system a lot longer than society teaches.

Marijuana is a huge problem with **Post-Acute Withdrawal Syndrome.** What people need to be more aware of is why people who try to give it up, especially in the first acute stage of withdrawal, do not make it. They just need to give it more time and go through the post-acute withdrawal stage.

The stigma is after 3 months of treatment, you come home from treatment and simple things can set you off. Your second and final stage of recovery emotional and psychological starts after 3 months, usually up to 1 year sometimes 2!

The final stage and that can take up to 1 or 2 years, generally symptoms will dissipate over time generally in the first 3 months to a year and you can live a more happy and healthy life!!

Just knowing about P.A.W.S. is helping me with my sobriety and educating myself about it and knowing what to expect is more than half of it. I wish I knew about it just 7 months ago.

I really want people to know if your struggling with addiction, please educate yourself about P.A.W.S..

It is very important and mentally you can be stronger fighting through whatever addiction you might have and just give it time.

Let time and your higher power do its magic and you can live a sober and prosperous life, worry free from addiction!

Resources

Alvernia University. (September 26, 2019), *Habit vs. Addiction: What's the Difference?* https://online.alvernia.edu/articles/habit-vs-addiction/

American Addiction Centers, (March 16, *2021)., Post-acute-withdrawal syndrome (P.A.W.S.): An in-depth guide.* Edited by Marisa Crane, B.S. https://americanaddictioncenters.org/withdrawal-timelines-treatments/post-acute-withdrawal-syndrome

Bhandari S., MD., (2019). *What Is Dopamine?* https://www.webmd.com/mental-health/what-is-dopamine

Bonnet U, Preuss UW. The cannabis withdrawal syndrome: current insights. *Subst Abuse Rehabil.* 2017; 8:9-37. doi:10.2147/SAR.S109576

Buddy, T., (2020). *Is P.A.W.S. real or just another relapse excuse? Post Acute withdrawal syndrome blamed for many relapses.* https://www.verywellmind.com/is-P.A.W.S.-real-or-another-relapse-excuse-4109902

Clancy, C. (2021), Habit vs. Addiction: 4 Questions To Determine The Difference. https://journeypureriver.com/habit-vs-addiction-4-questions-determine-difference/

Hartney, E., (November 5, 2021). *How Long Does Withdrawal From Marijuana Last?* https://www.verywellmind.com/what-to-expect-from-cannabis-withdrawal-22304

Mental Health Daily. (n.d.). *Post-acute withdrawal syndrome: causes, symptoms, treatment.* https://mentalhealthdaily.com/2015/06/12/post-acute-withdrawal-syndrome-causes-symptoms-treatment/

National Institute of Health. (2019), *Biology of Addiction: Drugs and Alcohol Can Hijack Your Brain.* https://newsinhealth.nih.gov/2015/10/biology-addiction

Parisi, T., (2020). *Post-Acute withdrawal syndrome (P.A.W.S.)* https://www.addictioncenter.com/treatment/post-acute-withdrawal-syndrome-P.A.W.S./

Pyramid Healthcare, Inc. (2016). What's the Difference Between a Habit and an Addiction? https://www.pyramidhealthcarepa.com/habit-or-addiction/

Suggest Viewing and Reading

"Addiction Neuroscience 101" on YouTube
   https://youtu.be/bwZcPwlRRcc
"How long does it take to start really feeling better after I stop drinking?" on YouTube https://youtu.be/499ajGowVqM
How to Cope with P.A.W.S. after Rehab
   https://www.advancedrecoverysystems.com/cope-P.A.W.S.-rehab/
High Sobriety: my year without booze - Kindle edition by Stark, Jill. Health, Fitness & Dieting Kindle eBooks @ Amazon.com.
   https://www.amazon.com/High-Sobriety-year-without-booze-ebook/dp/B00B4MDUEG
"How Long Does Withdrawal From Marijuana Last?"
   https://www.verywellmind.com/what-to-expect-from-cannabis-withdrawal-22304 Elizabeth Hartney, November 5, 2021.
Neuroplasticity: how the brain can heal itself - All In The Mind - ABC Radio National
   https://www.abc.net.au/radionational/programs/allinthemind/neuroplasticity-and-how-the-brain-can-heal-itself/6406736
Post-Acute Withdrawal Syndrome (P.A.W.S.) - Addiction Center
   https://www.addictioncenter.com/treatment/post-acute-withdrawal-syndrome-P.A.W.S./
Prayer May Reshape Your Brain And Your Reality: NPR
   https://www.npr.org/templates/story/story.php?storyId=104310443
"Why Do I Have Depression After Getting Sober?" on YouTube
   https://youtu.be/B7CYKgw-gfI

Printed in the USA
CPSIA information can be obtained
at www.ICGtesting.com
LVHW050528130524
779804LV00012B/788